How to Start An Elderly Home Care Business with the Change in Your Pocket

GWEN M. WALKER

Published by: Step Out on faith Publishing
P.O. Box 16977
Jackson, Ms 39236

Library of Congress Catalog Card Number   99-93189

ISBN 0-9672052-0-4

Printed in the United States of America

Dedication

This book is dedicated to my husband, Murphy Walker my soul mate and the greatest thing that ever happen to me, and who encouraged me to write this book.

It is also dedicated to my Mother Katie, Daughter Patricia, God-daughter Jowanza and Sweetie.

In Loving memory of my Grandson Murphy.

Acknowledgements

There is so much to be thankful for, first and foremost, thanks to the Lord for through him all things are possible.

I would like to thank my family for all their support. Also the employees and clients of Walker's Senior Citizen Home Care who played a part in the development of this book.

A special thanks to my husband, for believing in this book and me and to my sister and Brother-in-law Ann & Joe of Fayette, Mississippi for editing this book.

And finally, to you for purchasing and reading these words right now, who will go out and start your own business putting people back to work and taking control of your own financial destiny.

Table of Contents

Appendixes:

INTRODUCTION

So, you want to open an Elderly Home Care Business. Do you want to learn how? You are in the right place.

Yes, you can start a home care business with the change in your pocket. I know, because I did it myself. My starting capital was only a few hundred dollars, and change from my husband's pocket. This book has been in the making for a long time. It wasn't an easy book to get out.

You, probably already have a hunch than an elderly home care business is what you ought to do. Why else would you be reading this book? Maybe you have even started to research the idea. This book will show you how to go forward, how to turn your idea, dream, and concept into reality.

You do have an ace in the hole, this book. It will give you an edge over existing and potential competition. The advice in this book was garnered from my personal experience. I have included only what applies to starting this type of business. It is a road map that tells you among other things, how to get started, how to finance, and how to develop it.

This book is designed to help you start your business. Your determination and perseverance will determine how far you will go.

PREFACE

How to start an elderly home care business with the change in your pocket, is written primarily for individuals who want to start a *non-medical* home care business for *private pay.* However, the business principles are the same whether you are starting or improving an existing one.

It is a resource for anyone who wants to start, improve or expand their business, but are not sure how to do it, or where to begin. It describes how to get started, planning and implementing the plan and how to get finances.

The business plan guide identifies the questions that need to be answered in order to build a business. How to start an elderly service business with the change in your pocket, provides the tools necessary for you to understand and answer those questions.

This book is written in clear, non-technical language. It is packed with facts and techniques needed to:

- Make the initial decision to start your own business
- Plan, organize and finance
- Location of business
- Staff the business
- Launch the new business

•Ensure it viability

•Sustain both profitability and growth

Building a business today is not easy. It takes perseverance, resourcefulness, hard work, energy, independence, and it takes Knowledge. Many people have the traits, but lack the knowledge. If you are seeking the *know-how-to* build your business, this *book is for you*.

PART I

Agency Start-up

CHAPTER 1

Getting Started

The development and operation of an elderly home care business, requires that you have a little knowledge and experience in this type of business. It demands knowledge of federal, state, and local laws and regulations as they pertain to health and social service agencies. Information is needed regarding licensing, training, and other regulations that affect the delivery of this type of service. It is not necessary that you are a Registered Nurse, but you should have a nurse on staff to perform assessments and make home visits when necessary. Agencies who provide service under **Medicare/Medicaid must be licensed by the State with a Registered Nurse on staff.** To provide just Sitter service, a nurse is not required, but you should have some medical knowledge and know where the line is drawn as to the care you are allow to provide.

To start and run this type of business, you will need to wear many hats. When you run your business, you will be **Chief Executive, Marketing and Advertising Director, Personnel Manager, Bookkeeper,** and much more. Not all hats you will be wearing are going to fit well. So don't neglect a business task because you can't or don't want to handle it. You can either learn to do it, or hire someone to do it for you.

At the onset, you should become familiar with as many aspects of the services as possible. This will assist you in determining the need for the services offered. Contact major hospitals and social service agencies, to determine the number of requests for the type of services you will be offering.

While knowing the business is necessary for success, it isn't the only thing you need. The right **attitude** is equally important. The right attitude is the winner's attitude. It is a can do attitude.

So get ready for business success. Be clear about your goals and get motivated to accomplish them. Find out as much as possible about the elderly service business before attempting to open your doors. This can be done by getting additional education, talking to people in this field, take a job with another agency, research the business in the library, and so on. Even if this means delaying opening your business, it will be worthwhile, and you will be in a better position to keep it open.

As for those uncontrollable factors that also affect your business, the best way to deal with them is to stay tuned into what is happening in this area. Some people get caught up in their own affairs and fail to keep track of events that may have a direct bearing on their operation. You can avoid this by reading newspapers, listening to people, and observing the changes in your environment.

Steps to Follow When Getting Started

- Set your goals for the Agency
- Prepare Business Plan
- Estimate Star-up Cost
- Prepare Marketing Plan
- Choose what services to offer
- Set up Agency structure
- Develop Mission Statement
- Design and order business supplies
- Set fees for services
- Prepare Budget
- Select personnel needed
- Obtain license needed

Making The Decision

The decision to start a home care business should never be approached lightly. This is a major decision. Once you have committed yourself, you can be certain that the road ahead will be long, winding, and blocked by obstacles. If the business fails, and believe me it could, it may not only wreak havoc with your personal investment, but also with your ego.

I am not trying to discourage you from starting this business. But I am attempting to paint a realistic picture and foster caution on your part, because half of the businesses that start-up each year fail.

If you think that owing your own business, means working five-days a week from nine to five, leaving the office after eight hours, forgetting all about the office until the next working day, then this business is not for you. However, on the other hand, if you process a high level of confidence, think positively about the hard work, long hours, like challenges, then owning this kind of business may be right for you.

Before committing yourself to the investment of time, energy and money, it would make good sense to do a self-analysis, and some personal soul searching. Some people have difficulty seeing themselves in a realistic light. Many have overly inflated egos and believe they can do anything. Forget your natural modesty; yet do be honest with yourself evaluation.

Advantages and Disadvantages

Before you make the decision to start an elderly home care business, you should first analyze the advantages and disadvantages of starting this kind of business.

While there are many benefits to starting this kind of business, the advantages and disadvantages should be kept in mind. There are many reasons for going into business, some are logical, others are emotional, and a combination of the two.

ADVANTAGES:
1) Being your own boss
2) Job Security
3) Like what you are doing
4) Accumulate wealth
5)Pride in your accomplishment

DISADVANTAGES:
1) Lost of investment
2) Long hours
3) Fluctuation of income
4) Total responsibility
5) Pressures

Before you start, ask yourself if the advantages out weight the disadvantages? Are you willing to pay the price? These are questions only you can answer.

Next, ask yourself if you have what it takes to own this type of business? Some of the characteristics that are most important are: Motivation, confidence, risk taker, ability, to make decision, and good communication skills. The final decision is yours to make...............

Planning The Agency

Planning is setting goals and objectives, gathering resources like staff and money, a time-table, and a plan for monitoring the effectiveness. The plan is usually in writing.

Planning helps answer key questions:

• What will the agency do? • Needs of the seniors in the community • Types of services needed • Senior population • How will the agency carry out its mission?

Planning is a road map during the implementation phase, which can be used for grants and fundraising. Although you may be tempted to skip the planning steps, it will work better to complete them all. It is a continuous process, which agencies use to stay alert to the community needs. So expect to re-visit goals and objectives, budgets, policies, and marketing issues many times in the future.

Assessment: Essential part of planning. It provides valuable information about the needs of seniors. Information such as the types of services needed or the number of seniors in need can be used in planning your agency.

Remember, that planning is a continuous changing and often-disorderly process. As you gain new information during planning you may want to re-visit and adjust previously made decisions.

CHAPTER 2

Agency Structure

After weighing the advantages and disadvantages of starting this type of business, your next step is to decide whether to go forward. Starting this type of business is like deciding whether or not to have a child, they require twenty-four hours a day dedication, and both can bring you great joy.

As you go through the process of starting this business this is the point you need to make the decision about the legal structure, which is best for you. The structure you select will determine how your business will be taxed, raising money, whether you will be personally liable for its debts, and how much paperwork you will have to do.

There are three basic forms of businesses: They are *Sole Proprietorship, Partnership, and Corporations.*

9

There are some issues you should consider as you make your decision: 1) Who gets to make the decisions that affects the business? 2) How are taxes assessed, who is responsible for paying them and how much must be paid? 3) Who is liable if the business loses money, or even worse goes bankrupt?

Each form has its advantages and disadvantages; you must consider the trade-off, as you make your decision as to which form is right for you.

While you must choose one form to get started, you can change to a different one once your business grows and changes. This decision should not be made lightly, but it is not written in stone for the life of your business.

Sole Proprietorship

Sole Proprietorship: A business form in which one individual owns the business. This is by far the easier, least expensive, least complicated way to start and run a business. About 90% of all American small businesses fit in this category.

As a sole proprietorship, you are in the driver's seat. In addition to having total control over your business, you have total responsibility for it. Just as all profits will be yours, so will all its debts and liabilities.

Sole proprietorship has two options of operating: under your own name or a *fictitious name*. However, the word corporation cannot be included in the fictitious name. Sole proprietorship, is not taxed as a separate entity, but is reported on Schedule C, filed with the owner's tax return.

Advantages of Sole Proprietorship

1) You are the Boss: The freedom to run the business any way you chooses; the ability to make decisions quickly without having to wait for committee approval. If you are looking for maximum control, limited government interference, the sole proprietorship could be just the thing.

2) It is easy to Start: Sole proprietorship is by far the simplest form to choose. There is no red tape, all you need is the assets and commence operations.

3) You Keep all Profits: All profits go to the owner; you are not obligated to share with anyone.

4) Income is taxed as personal income by IRS: Income derived from this form of business is considered part of the owner's income. You can deduct the losses from your personal tax.

5) You can close the business at will: If you decide to close the business and move on to something new, it is quite simple; you need only to cease operation.

Disadvantages of Sole proprietorship

1) Assume unlimited liability: Sole proprietorship owner is responsible for all business debts or legal judgments against the business. Your own personal assets, home, automobile and saving can be claimed by creditors. This unlimited liability is the sole proprietorship worst feature.

2) The investment capital you raise is limited: The amount of investment capital you can raise is limited to the money you have to borrow. Unlike partnership or corporations, which can draw on the resources of others, sole proprietorship has to provide the total investment for their business.

3) **You need to be a Generalist**: Anyone who starts a sole proprietorship must be prepared to perform a variety of functions ranging from accounting to advertising.

4) **Retaining high Caliber employees is difficult**: You may have difficulty in holding onto your best employees because they want more than you are offering them. For those employees a good salary and bonus usually won't be enough. Your only resources are to let them go or to convert your sole proprietorship into a partnership.

5) **The Life of the Business is limited**: The death of the owner automatically terminates a sole proprietorship, as does any unforeseen circumstances that keep the owner from operating the business.

PARTNERSHIP

A *partnership,* exist when two or more people share in the ownership of a business. By agreement, they determine the amount of time and money each partner will invest in the business and the percentage of the profits each will receive. The extent of each partner authority and liability must also be made clear.

To avoid any misunderstanding later, everything that has been agreed to should be in writing. An Attorney can be helpful with this. The importance of a written partnership agreement cannot be over emphasized. In the absence of such a document, the courts resolve any dispute that arises but the outcome might not be to your liking.

Here is some information that should be included in your partnership agreement:

- •Each partner's responsibilities and authority

- •The extent of each partner's liability

- •The amount of capital each will invest

- •How profits and losses are to be shared

- •Type of partnership

- •How assets are distributed if business is dissolved

- •Withdrawal and admission of partners

Advantages of A Partnership

1) **Two heads are better than one:** In a partnership you have the advantages of being able to draw on the skills and abilities of each partner.

2) **It is easy to get started**: Starting a partnership is relatively easy. Although it entails additional cost and more planning than a sole proprietorship, red tape is minimal.

3) **More investment capital is available**: Your business ability to increase capital can be enhanced by simply bringing in more partners.

4) **Partnership pays only personal income tax:** They are taxed the same as sole proprietorship. The total income of the business is considered to be the personal income of the partners. This means there is no separate business income tax to pay, and business losses are deductible from each partner's income tax.

5) Employees can be made partners: Partnership is able to attract and retain high caliber employees by offering them the opportunity to become partners.

Disadvantages of A Partnership

1) Partners have unlimited liability: Like sole proprietorship, partners are responsible for all debts or legal judgments against the business.

2) Profits must be shared: All profits resulting from the partnership must be distributed among the partners in accordance with the partnership agreement.

3) The Partners may disagree: Disputes among partners can literally destroy a partnership.

4) The life of the business is limited: As with a sole proprietorship, the life of a partnership is limited. Should one of the partners withdraw, die, or become ill to carry on, the partnership is automatically dissolved. Although it is possible for the remaining partners to reorganize the business, the financial interest of the departing partner must be paid. Furthermore, anytime a new partner is admitted to the business, dissolution and the addition of the new partner must be formed.

There are different forms of partnerships, such as General Partnership and Limited Partnership and Registered Limited Liability Partnership.

General Partnership- A partnership exists when two or more persons join together in the operation and management of a business venture. It is like a sole proprietorship subject to relatively little regulation and is fairly easy to establish. A formal partnership agreement is recommended in order to address potential conflicts before they arise: for example, who will be responsible for performing each task, what, if any consultation is needed between partners before major decisions are made, if a partner dies, and so on. Under general partnership each partner is liable for all debts of the business. All profits are taxed as income to the partners based on their percentage of ownership. A general partnership registers a business name with the county city clerk's office in which the business is located.

General Partnership Requirements

- Partnership must consist of at least two persons
- Partnership agreement may be "verbal" or "written" and filed.
- Each partner must contribute effort (service) and or resources (assets).

- Association between partners must be consensual

- Profit and Losses must be shared.

Limited Partnership- Like a general partnership a limited partnership is established by an agreement between two or more individuals. In a limited, however, there are two types of partners. A general partner has greater control in some aspects of the partnership, for instance; only a general partner can decide to dissolve the partnership. General partners have no limitations on the dividends they can receive from profit and so incur unlimited liability. Limited partners can only receive a share of profits based on the prorated amount on their investment, and the liability is similarly limited in proportion to their investment.

Limited Partnership Requirements

- File an application with the secretary of State which must contain:
- Name and Taxpayer ID number
- Address of the principal place of business
- Name and address of each partner
  The name of the partnership must clearly state in its name language that it is a limited partnership.
- There must be at least one general partner.

Registered Limited Liability Partnership – It is designed to provide partners with insulation from liability arising from the acts of other partners of partnership agents. The RLLP is formed by converting a pervious existing partnership by filing an application with the Secretary of State stating the name of the partnership, its address and principle office, number of partners, and a statement of the business in which the partnership engages, and executed by a majority of the partners. Again, the purpose of the RLLP is to provide protection of partners from the errors and omissions of other partners in the organization.

CORPORATION

A Corporation differs from other legal forms of business in that the laws considers it to be an artificial being, possessing the same rights and responsibilities as a person. Unlike a sole proprietorship or a partnership, a corporation has an existence separate from its owners. As such, it can sue and be sued, own property, agree to contracts, and engage in business transactions. Additionally, since a corporation is a separate entity, it is not dissolved with every change in ownership. The results of this are that corporations have the potential for unlimited life.

ADVANTAGES OF INCORPORATING:

- Limits liability of shareholders, including the owners to the amount each has invested.
- Offers continuity when business owner or owners die or are disabled.
- Allows the separation of business functions based on the skills and abilities of the principles.
- Allows flexibility in the transfer of ownership

DISADVANTAGES OF INCORPORTING

- Is expensive to launch
- Is more heavily taxed than other business forms
- Limits power to charter
- Provides less freedom of activity for owners
- Have strict legal formalities and regulations

THE CORPORATE CHARTER

To form a corporation you must be granted a charter by the State in which you live. Each State sets its requirements and fees for the issuance of charters.

STOCKHOLDERS

Each person who owns stock in your corporation is a co-owner with you in the business. This does not mean that every stockholder will actively participate in your company, or even be associated with it in any way, other than by purchasing shares of the corporation stocks.

THE BOARD OF DIRECTORS

The Board of Directors represents the stockholders and is responsible for protecting their interest. Board members are elected annually, usually for one-year, which can be renewed indefinitely by means of the election process.

The Board of Directors generally concerns itself with determining corporate policies, rather than taking care of the daily operations.

TYPES OF CORPORATIONS

"C" Corporation- Is a legal entity made up of persons who have received a Charter legally recognizing the corporation as a separate entity having its own rights, privileges and liabilities, apart from those of the individuals forming the corporation. It is the most complex form of business organization and is comprised of three groups of people; shareholders, directors, and officers. The corporation can own assets, borrow money and perform business functions without directly involving the owner(s) of the corporation.

The corporation therefore is subject to more government regulations than sole proprietorship or partnership. Its earnings are subject to "double taxation" when the corporation is taxed and then passed through as stockholder dividends. However, corporations have the advantages of limited liability, but not total protection from lawsuits. Shares are publicly traded on a securities exchange; organized under general corporate codes.

SUBCHAPTER "S" CORPORATION

-is a type of corporation specially suited to small business. It is generally treated like a corporation for legal purposes, but like a partnership for income-taxed purposes. Its income is taxed to the shareholders as if the corporation were a partnership.

NONPROFIT CORPORATION

– Are presumed to be charitable in nature, the law grants special privileges. It is the Government way of paying these organizations back for their contributions to the general welfare of the public.

A nonprofit corporation is exempt from income tax. You must apply to IRS for 501©3 status, and you must file Articles of Incorporation with the State where the business is incorporated.

PROFESSIONAL CORPORATION

- Individuals who are licensed in certain professions may form a professional corporation. This provides them with the benefits of a corporate structure for the business aspects of the practice while preserving the personal professional relationship between them and the clients they serve.

CHAPTER **3**

Forming
The Agency

You have made the decision to start the business, have weighted the advantages and disadvantages, and decided what form of business you want.

Next, the steps to take are: name your business; get licenses; file for EIN; choose an office location; furniture and equipment; design and order business cards.

CHOOSING AGENCY NAME

The choice of your agency's name is one of the most important decisions you will make, and the one with the lowest cost.

The name you choose can be an important sales tool and critical factor in developing a positive image or it can be a source of confusion to prospects and even to clients.

You can put as little or too much into a name you choose, but the choice you make will have a bearing on how hard or easy it will be for you to market your business.

STEPS TO CREATING AGENCY NAME

- Generate a long list of words, which describe what you want your agency to reflect.

- Piece those words together....play with them

- Review your creation in relation to what you know about the people who would be using your services.

- Select the best name you have created

- Make sure the name you select meets most of what your business does.

FICTITIOUS AGENCY NAME

If you are planning to operate under a name other than your own, then you will need to file a *fictitious name statement* with the City Clerk of Court. The purpose of this statement is to inform the public of your identity and the identities of any others who are Co-Owners in the business. *See sample*.

FICTITIOUS BUSINESS NAME STATEMENT

File No_____   The following person is doing business as

1. Fictitious Business Name_____

2.

_____

Street Address,   City   State
Zip Code

3.Full name of Registrant_____

_____

_____

Residence Address

4. Check only one: This business is conducted by (   ) an individual   (   ) partnership   (   ) an incorporate association other than a partnership (   ) a business trust (   ) Co-partners   (   ) husband and wife   (   ) joint venture   (   ) Other

5.   THE REGISTRANT COMMENCED TO TRANSACT BUSINESS UNDER THE FICTITIOUS BUSINESS NAME LISTED ABOVE ON:
Date:

Notice: This fictitious name statement expires five years from the date it was filed in the clerk office. A new fictitious business name statement must be filed before that time. The filing of this statement does not of itself authorize the use in this state of a fictitious business name in violation of the rights of any other under federal, state, or common law

6. Signature_____

_____
Type or print name

If Registrant is a corporation sign below
Corporation
Name_____
Signature
Title_____

23

BUSINESS OR OCCUPATIONAL LICENSE

To maintain set standards of performance and protect the safety of consumers, most States regulate entry into specific occupations or professions, such as those in health care services.

Business license are issued by the city's in which the business is located and is usually valid for one year. You can obtain applications from the cities business license office.

If you plan on providing service under Medicare or Medicaid, you will need to contract the department of health and hospitals in your area, and meet the requirement set forth by the State Licensing board.

EMPLOYER IDENTIFICATION NUMBER
EIN

If you employ one or more persons in your business, the Federal Government requires you to have an employer identification number. This enables the Government to verify that you are paying all appropriate employer taxes and withholding the proper amount from employee's paychecks.

At the beginning you may not have any employees; it is still advisable to obtain EIN number. And if you should decide to hire someone later, take in a partner, or incorporate, you will need the number for tax purposes.

Obtaining your EIN number is an easy matter. There is no fee for it. Just call IRS at 1-800-829-3676 and request form SS-4. On the web you can reach them at irs.gov and print your form.

STATE UNEMPLOYMENT NUMBER

You will need to apply with the State Department of Labor Office in your area to be assigned a number. You will need this number to file your quarterly reports and for the end of the year W-2's for employees.

STATE INDENTIFICATION NUMBER

You will also need a State ID number, to report and file State taxes for your employees. You can obtain that number from the State Labor office in your area.

STATE BOARD OF NURSING ADMINISTRATOR

Apply to the *State Board of Nurse Aide Registry*, to be assigned a facility code number. You will need to file a yearly report on all nurse aide you have working.

BUSINESS LOCATION

Proper office location is both a marketing and operation decision. Your ideal location should fit the business image, be of ample size and layout to meet your needs, zoned for this type of business, and priced within your budget.

To day many people are operating their business out of the home. It is an inexpensive way to get started, and you may find that it helps you meet some personal goals. To determine whether it make sense for you, ask yourself the following questions: will working out of my home negatively impact the image of my business in the eyes of my clients? Do I have the space in my home to create a separate office?

By the way, I started working my business from my home and did very well. But because of family who did not take my business seriously and would say things like, "you don't have a real business", also some of the employees felt the same way when they would come to the office. I moved to an office outside my home, and found the perceptions of my business changed, and my expenses increased substantially.

After ten years in an office outside my home, I finally realized I am the same person, and my business was sold because of me not where my office was located. My husband built me a beautiful office; I move my business back to my home and continued to do very well. My clients did not care where my office was located, only the services I provided.

If there is no way you can use part of your home as a office, then you will need to rent an office that is convenient for you rather than the clients.

ELEMENTS OF YOUR BUSINESS IDENTITY

LOGO: A logo is a distinctive graphic element either a symbol or arrangement of letters, that represents your business. It can provide instant recognition. A well- designed logo also imparts an air of professionalism to all the printed material of your business.

BUSINESS CARDS: Your business card set the tone for how your business is perceived. Regardless of the identity you want to convey, it's important to make sure that your cards reflects an appropriate level of professionalism as well. In addition to your business name and address, make sure your name and business telephone number is on the card.

LETTERHEAD AND
MATCHING ENVELOPES

As with your business cards, people are going to make judgments about your business based on the identity your stationary projects. You can help ensure that they perceive the identity you're trying to project, by having a uniform appearance throughout your printed materials. A good way to do this is to make sure you have your stationary and business cards printed as a package. Always include your business address, telephone number and fax number on letterhead to give people every opportunity to get in touch with you.

NOTE: Don't go overboard on business cards and stationary. You can have a very impressionable business card without succumbing to expensive gimmicks and flashy designs. The money you will spend on gimmicks can be better spent developing your business. The one thing you might consider spending money on is developing your logo for your agency. This will communicate a sense of stability to your clients.

CHAPTER 4

Change In
Your Pocket

Yes, you can start your business with the change in your pocket. However, you cannot live off the business for the first year or beyond. You will need other sources of income to pay your personal living expenses. There are three potential sources for living expenses: spouses' wages, your savings, or wages from another job you hold down while launching your new business on the side.

I was lucky, to have a husband who worked full-time, so we could live off his salary. If you are the only moneymaker in your household, and do not have a great deal of saving, you can start the business part-time. This is often the alternative of choice.

HOW MUCH WILL IT COST
TO GET STARTED

This is the first question, most people ask when thinking about starting a business. Estimating how much money you need to start your business is difficult and frustrating. It always takes longer than you think, you are not sure if the numbers you are dealing with are accurate.

In the first section, we will estimate all the one-time start-up cost you are going to have before you can get to opening day. The next section we will look at is working capital, the money you need to keep the business open.

START-UP COST

DEPOSITS:

If you are renting office space, you are going to need deposits for the telephone, utility, insurance, not to mention your landlord. However, if you are working from home, you will only need to deal with the phone company.

STATIONARY:

Go to a professional printer and get yourself some simple business cards; black and white with your logo if you have one, plus your name on the cards. Do the same with letterhead and envelopes, but do not order too much. Don't think that a large supply of stationary or a closet full of supplies signifies that you are a *"real business"*.

PERSONNEL:

You may need to hire additional help for the office, or maybe a family member can help.

OFFICE EQUIPMENT:

Your needs will be very particular, so I am only going to discuss equipment briefly. The first thing you will want is to sort out your telephone needs. You can't afford to allow customers to hear a busy signal, so you will need to get call waiting, or if you can afford it a two line phone. Business rates are expensive about two to three times more than a home phone.

You will also need a decent telephone. You want to buy a solid looking telephone, one that can stand a shower or coffee or a fall to the floor. If you have two lines you will need one that can be put on hold.

There are two other related products you will need: an answering machine and most likely a fax machine. You should invest in a good answering machine, and make sure you can call in and get your messages easily. A fax machine is not necessary, you must decide what you are going to use it for, and then buy the model that best fits your needs.

Next, you will need a computer. You will have to make the decision as to the best kind and what you can afford to pay for one. If you cannot afford the computer at this time, you can use a typewriter. If you do not have either a typewriter or computer, you can go to the library or your local copy center and use theirs. Shop around for the best bargain.

To help you understand how I started with the change in my pocket, I have included my start-up cost. On the next page is a sample start-up cost for my agency. What follows is a record of everything I actually spent. This will give you an idea of what your start-up costs might look like.

SAMPLE START-UP COST FOR
W.S.C HOME HEALTH CARE AGENCY

I.   RENT AND DEPOSITS:

I rented an office for $350.00 a month and paid a $350.00 deposit. I ask the landlord to split the deposit into 3-payments and she agreed. I had to pay $100.00 utility deposit for the gas and electric.

II.   OFFICE EQUIPMENT:

I needed to put in a new telephone line, buy a new phone and answering machine. I owned a typewriter, computer and printer so I did not have to buy them. I bought a used file cabinet and desk. I used a lot of furniture I had at my house that I was not using any more.

III.   STATIONARY:

I went to a local printer and ordered some business cards. I liked the results, so I ordered letterheads and envelopes to match.

1,000 business cards.................$46.00

500 letterhead/envelopes......... 66.00

IV.   SIGN:

I had a sign printed to place on the outside of my office building. The cost was $110.00

V.   INSURANCE

I purchase liability insurance for both the business and the property. The landlord usually wants insurance to protect the property.

VI.   LICENSES:

I paid for occupational license with the city and license from the State.

VII.   OFFICE PERSONNEL:

I was blessed with a lady name Gloria, who worked for no pay. She worked just a hard as if she was getting paid. When I was able to pay her, she became ill and had to stop working. But for three years she worked hard and long hours with me. I will forever be grateful to her.

It may be possible for you to find someone who can help you in the office with answering the phone, taking applications, etc. for little or no pay in the beginning.

HERE IS A BREAKDOWN OF WHAT IT ACTUALLY COST ME TO OPEN FOR BUSINESS

Office Rent	$350.00
Office Deposit	216.00
Equipment	300.00
Stationary	112.00
Sign	110.00
Insurance	194.00
Licenses	100.00
Office Personnel	0

TOTAL START-UP COST $1,382.00

Bear in mind, that had I been starting a different kind of business or *working from home*, the start-up cost would have been a lot less. **The start-up cost may look something like this:**

Rent	0
Deposits	0
Office equipment	300.00
Stationary	112.00
Sign	0
Insurance	100.00
License	100.00

TOTAL START-UP COST $612.00

WHERE DID I GET THE START-UP FUNDS?

Well, my husband and I both had a habit of putting our coins in a jar. So one day I counted the coins and found that we had over $400.00 in coins. Then we had some saving bonds, so I cashed them in early. I used my credit card to pay for stationary, sign and office equipment. So that is how I covered the $1,382.00 to open my business.

WORKING CAPITAL

So, far, we have looked at what it cost to start-up your business. Now, we will look at what will be needed to keep the business open until you start making money or rather making a profit from your business. This is called *Working Capital.*

WHAT IS WORKING CAPITAL?

Working capital is the money you will need to tide the business over until it makes enough money to cover its own monthly and yearly costs. Another way to think of working capital is the temporary funds for your business.

WHERE DO YOU GET WORKING CAPITAL?

This is the point, where you will need to feed money into the business. So, if you don't have any saving, you will need to generate cash to put into the business. It takes a service business a while to start receiving cash in, because you are not selling products you are selling services. Each month you will have costs you must meet, like rent and phone bill.

I am going to briefly look at some ways you can get financing. In order to raise money for start-up, you must have some of your own invested. If you are not risking your life saving then no one takes you seriously.

WAYS TO FINANCE YOUR BUSINESS

BANKS: You are not at the stage where they are willing to lend a small business like yours money for start-up. That is why I advise you not to waste your time it is not worth it.

If you have a saving account with money in it, you can borrow against the amount you have in it. They will hold your saving as collateral for the loan. Keep in mind you cannot use money in the saving if you get a loan against it.

PARTNERSHIP: You can form a partnership with another person, who will invest in the business and share ownership. *Be careful, this could be risky.*

HOME EQUITY LOAN: If you own property, this is the most popular way to raise capital, because for most people the home is the largest untapped resources available.

FAMILY and FRIENDS: Ask them for whatever financial help they can loan you. You may not need to sell yourself to them they already know you. But you will need to show them what you are doing. I want to emphasize this option, because it's the way many small businesses get started. You need to be clear about these questions before you move in this direction. What if you fail? How badly will you hurt your personal relationship if your business falls through?

YOUR OWN MONEY: No one likes to hear this one, but you will be amazed at how much money you can save if you put your mind to it. Such as: stop eating out, cut down on your drinking, don't buy new clothes, disconnect cable, and cut down on grocery bill.

GRANTS: There are no grants to start a business of this kind. If you luck out and find one, the criteria's are very strict and you need to be able to write a mind blowing good proposal in order to be considered.

LIFE INSURANCE: You can borrow money against your life insurance polices.

CREDIT CARD: Use your credit cards to purchase what you need to start your business.

ARRANGE CREDIT: Try to arrange credit with your suppliers. They maybe willing to provide supplies you need today and allow you to pay for it with interest over the next six months.

COMMUNITY PROGRAMS: Be aware of what is happening in your community. There are a variety of State and Local programs in almost every community in the United States to provide special financing for small businesses.

SMALL BUSINESS ADMINISTRATION (SBA)

They help low-income minority and women to get business loans. The loans for amounts less than $10,000, but under some conditions can be up to $25,000 and are to be used for working capital, inventory, supplies, and equipment.

NET WORK: These are people out there willing to help you, but you never know who they are; where they will turn up; or how they will provide help. Let people know what you are trying to do.

FUND RAISING EVENTS: Garage sales, suppers, raffles

START SMALL and GROW: You may need to start small, but that's far better than never getting off the ground. Instead of asking question: How much do I need to start? Ask, what can I successfully do with the cash I can get? You can always grow later after you have achieved some measure of success.

By using one or a combination of these methods you should be able to raise some working capital. **Be patient, but be persistent and professional. You will find money somewhere.**

PART II

PLANNING FOR SUCCESS

CHAPTER 5

The Systematic Way to Success

Success in business, or in anything else, is a matter of accomplishment...... of getting things done. Your business success is measured by how well you do what you set out to do.

Proper planning is necessary to ensure your success. You should start by defining your mission, setting your goals, both long term and short term. This will give you a clear vision of what you want to achieve.

MISSION STATEMENT

A *mission statement* provides a long term vision of what the agency is striving to become. Ideally, mission statements are written in terms narrow enough to provide practical guidance, yet broad enough to stimulate creative thinking.

A well thought out written mission statement, provides everyone in the agency particularly *home care* personnel with a shared sense of purpose, direction, and achievement. The mission statement communicates to managers and employees the reasons for being an agency.

CREATING A MISSION STATEMENT

Creating a mission statement can be as simple as answering the questions: What business are we in? What services do we want to provide? What will we be allowed to do? Do we have the resources to do it? What does the community need?

Before a home care agency can develop an effective market plan, the mission of the agency must be defined.

EXAMPLE OF A MISSION STATEMENT

The purpose of Walker's Home Care is to provide essential social services to Senior's in our community, to enable them to stay in their home and avoid premature entry into Nursing Homes.

GOAL SETTING

As a business owner you may become task oriented. You will get caught up in the day- to- day activities of running the business, instead of focusing on what you are trying to accomplish. You may feel you don't have the time to set goals. However, successful business owners make the time to plan because they know how crucial it is to obtain success.

A *goal* is different than a wish or a hope. Wishing and hoping are passive, dreamy states of mind without power. A goal on the other hand is conscious and active. Goal setting produces positive results in a number of ways. First, having a goal focuses your attention causing you to think about the goal more and become more aware of opportunities related to it. Next, goals also provide a criterion of making important decisions and a reference point for planning.

Each goal is a clearly defined objective to be reached at some specific time in the future. When you accomplish the goal within the specified time frame, you are successful with regard to that goal.

GOAL SETTING IN BUSINESS

What works for your personal life, works for business too. The specific business goals you set will depend on your business and your definition of success. Some of the more common types of business goals are: increase in sales, profits, gross margins, to name a few.

It is difficult to overstate how critical the goal setting process is to business success. Setting and accomplishing goals, keep a business moving in the right direction. Without goals there isn't an objective way to determine whether the business is successful or not.

HOW TO SET GOALS

Setting goals is the surest way to get from where you are, to where you want to be. But a goal is more than a desire, wish or hope. To work most powerful, a goal must be as follows:

Specific: The more precisely you define your goals, the easier it is to achieve. Saying you want your business to be successful isn't going to get you far. What exactly do you mean by successful?

Measurable: Goals expressed in numbers make it easy to measure your progress. Making your goals measurable also ensures that they are specific. Dollars are the numbers that often measure business success.

Time Frame: Having a definite date for you to accomplish goals provides the context for judging success. At the end of the month, quarter, or year, measure your actual results against the goals you had set to determine whether you have succeeded in accomplishing them.

Written: Until goals are written down, they don't have any power. Once they are committed to paper, they become a reference point you can keep referring back to. The act of expressing your goals tangibly in writing gives them the power of conviction.

Planned Out: Develop a strategy for achieving your main objective. Develop an overall plan that includes the most essential steps for achieving the goals. Assign a time frame for each short-term goal. Identify resources that can help you achieve your goals. Anticipate possible obstacles and develop a plan for dealing with them.

Monitor: Periodically review your results. When the results fall short of your goals, identify any problem areas and take corrective action. If your actions are working, keep on doing the same thing. But if they are not working, then try something else. Monitoring goals daily or weekly gives you more opportunity to gauge your progress. Frequent monitoring keeps you on track.

LONG-TERM GOALS

Long-Term Goals: are those things you want to accomplish three or more years into the future. They include sales, profit, and competitive position goals. The goals set for the current year should be designed to facilitate the accomplishment of your long-term goals.

Use your long-term business goals as the foundation for your business planning. When setting goals get your employees and associates involved in the process, they will be more committed to achieving the goals if they had a role in setting them.

SHORT-TERM GOALS

In order to accomplish your long term goals, you have to break them down into short-term goals. A three year goal would be broken into three one-year goals. Then each of the yearly goals would be broken down into twelve monthly goals, which could be subdivided into weekly goals and finally into daily goals.

As each of the smaller sub-goals are accomplished, you move closer to accomplishing your long-term goals. Use a planning calendar, daily to do list, and project schedule to keep track of your goals.

SEEING THE BIG PICTURE

When choosing your log-term goals, it is a good idea to view the future of your business in terms of THE BIG PICTURE. No business operates in isolation, each one is part of an industry, economy, and society. That's why business decisions have to take in much more than just what is happening at the present time.

Seeing the big picture is a good motto for judging whether your efforts are achieving your goals. But before setting your goals, you should realize that the reverse is also true, when it comes to business, believing is seeing.

Keep in mind as you plan for the future, that circumstances do not remain the same; expand your vision to include innovations and trends instead of resisting them. Make sure your beliefs are based on what is actually happening. If they are, the goals you set will be much more likely to be accomplished.

CHAPTER 6

Business Plan

A *Business Plan* often seems a matter of luck, or even magical, to many business owners. They don't realize that there is usually a critical differences between those businesses that succeed and those that fail. Often that make or break difference is a business plan. Without a plan, a business can easily flounder and fall victim to poor business decisions resulting from a lack of planning.

A well- prepared business plan serves at least three critical functions: *Getting the business started off right; A blueprint for success; and raising money.*

It should be written specifically to the audience for whom it is intended. When a business plan is in the formative stages, the business plan should be written to aid you in making sound decisions for getting the business up and running. Once the business is operating, the plan should be written to convey your vision to employees and others who are helping you achieve your dream. It should be a step-by- step recipe for what is going to be done and who will do it.

WHY WRITE A BUSINESS PLAN?

Writing a business plan will help you discover a great deal about whether your idea is likely to succeed. If you don't write a plan you won't know whether your business idea is a good one until after the business is open and then it is too late.

A business plan helps you think through the strategies, balance your enthusiasm with the facts, and recognize your limitations. It will help you avoid potentially disastrous errors, like negative cash flow, hiring the wrong people and the wrong market.

Your business plan will also help if you need to borrow money. The plan is the heart and soul of your business and the most important set of documents provided by you to any lending institution or investor.

In short the business plan:

- Sells you on the business

- Sells others on the business

- Gives you confidence

- Improves your chances of success

WHAT YOUR BUSINESS PLAN SHOULD INCLUDE

There is no right way to organize and write a business plan. But every business plan should convey the following:

- Table of contents
- Cover sheet
- Executive Summary
- Services offered

- Market analysis
- Operations plan
- Sales plan
- Management plan
- Financial data
- Appendixes
- Other supporting documents

COVER SHEET: The cover sheet should be neat, attractive, and short. It should identify the business, location, telephone number, and the person who wrote the business plan.

EXECUTIVE SUMMARY: Executive summary is the heart of the business plan. This portion of the plan must be designed to capture and hold the interest of the person that the plan is being presented. It is also the only portion of the plan that everyone who see it is sure to read. Make it good! Keep it between two to five pages of typed copy.

This summary is an overview of the entire business. It will demonstrate that you are focused on your goals, what you want, and where you are going.

SERVICES OFFERED: Here is where you describe your services and what makes it special. Emphasize the difference between what is on the market and what services your agency will market. How much you will charge for the services.

MARKET ANALYSIS: The design of this section is to present sufficient facts to convince the reader of the business plan, that your services have a substantial market, and can achieve sales in the face of competition. Therefore, in writing this section you should begin by first systematically creating a broad base of information on your market. Then narrow your range of inquiry to focus on specific markets for your services, and evaluate your agency's potential for developing these markets.

A.   Description of the total market.

One way to define the total market is to list all the important characteristics using data from industry trade associations or government census sources. Find out what extent these characteristics are present in different areas.

B.   Target Market

Your target market, the market you have selected to serve, must be measured as above.

C.   Industry Trends

Describe the projections and trend for the industry

D.   Competition

At present who are your major competitors? How large are they compared to your business? How are they similar, dissimilar to your business? Where do you believe you have a business advantage? What are your competitors, strengths and weakness?

OPERATION PLAN: A service business should pay particular attention and focus on an appropriate location and ability to minimize overhead, lease the required equipment and obtain competitive productivity from a skilled trained labor force.

> •Location: What are the characteristics of your present location?
> •Physical Facility: How much space and what structural features do you require?

•Capital Equipment: Requires and evaluation of fixtures, furniture, and equipment.

•Availability of Labor: What is the labor market area? What skills are available in this market?

SALES PLAN: State the methods that your agency will use to create sales and to describe the service. Pricing, advertising, and distribution should all be included.

- Pricing policy: What price will the agency charge for each type of service.
- Distribution strategy: What is the geographic location of the potential consumer market?
- Promotion strategy: Describe the approaches your agency will use to bring your service to the attention of the target customers.

MANAGEMENT PLAN: This section includes the personal history of the owners, work experience, duties, responsibilities, salaries, organizational chart and sources available to the business.

- What is the personal history of the owners?
- What related work experience do they have?
- What are the duties of the owners?
- What is the compensation packet for owners?
- What other resources are available to the business?

FINANCIAL DATA: Projection or forecasts are an integral part of your financial data and are critical to accurately evaluate the feasibility of your venture and to plan the size of the investment required to achieve a stable level of operation. Your assumptions must be carefully though out and explained. Be honest for your own benefit. Over optimism can lead to failure.

- Balance Sheet: Show how the assets, liabilities and net worth of the agency are distributed at a given point.
- Income Statement: Submit a three-year projection summary.
- Cash flow Statement: Show how much cash will be required, when it will be needed, and what will be the source of funds.

As I stated previously, there is more than one way to write a business plan. The only thing that really counts is if the plan does what it is supposed to do... sell you and others who support you need.

CHAPTER 7

Marketing

Marketing must be an integral part of any successful business. It provides a client oriented focus that forces the agency to identify and meet the client needs.

Good marketing cannot guarantee the agency success, but it does substantially enhance the probability of success. Virtually every agency failure can be traced to a lack of good marketing, the lack of identifying and meeting the prospective client's needs.

Marketing is one of the most important phases of the business. It is impossible to cover all areas of marketing in this chapter. However, more information about marketing services is offered in my book...... Marketing Strategies.

DEFINITION OF MARKETING

Marketing is the process or mind set that focuses the agency's efforts and actions on identifying and meeting the client's needs and wants. It is not selling. Selling is a part of marketing however marketing is a lot more than selling. The terms are often used interchangeably. To market services for a home care agency, you must do more than sell. You must provide a viewpoint from which to integrate the agency, analyzing, planning, implementation, and control of the home care delivery system.

MARKETING SERVICES

There are differences between marketing services and marketing products. Certain features of services make them more difficult to market than products. They are intangible, perishable, and inseparable from the service provider and variable in quality.

Let's consider each quality:

Intangible: Buyer cannot touch, feel or handle as they can do with products. A service is rendered; it cannot be stored on a shelf, touched, tasted, or tried on for size.

Perishable: Services cannot be stored or warehoused. Thus a service business may experience a lost of sales because it lacks reserve to draw on.

Inseparable: This fact alone standardization of services become nearly impossible. It makes is difficult for potential buyers to "shop around", since the quality of service depends on the people involved. Thus the need for capable and well-trained personnel is quite evident.

Because of the distinctive characteristics of services, certain aspects of marketing then take on added importance. Two of the most important, are the capabilities of the people who perform or deliver services and the environment in which services take place.

MARKETING MIX

Every agency must be able to differentiate itself from competitors. After all, if your services are no different than another, why would a client choose your agency instead of the other? However, agencies do not offer to the public a tangible product such as an automobile, rather an agency's product is the combination of services offered.

A **marketing mix** is the mixture of controllable market that the agency uses to pursue the sought level of sales in the target market. The combination of those variables is unique to an individual. It is the marketing mix that differentiates your agency from any other agency that offers the same services.

The marketing mix consists of what is called the 4-p's: price, promotion, place and personnel. Developing a marketing mix for your agency is critical to the success of the agency. Describing the agency marketing mix is no different from describing yourself to a friend. Just as the description of yourself, the focus is what makes you unique, the same is true for the agency marketing mix.

THE 4-P'S
(PRICE, PROMOTION, PLACE, PERSONNEL)

PRICE: is closely related to specific services. The pricing of the agency must be explored. Is it nonprofit or a money making agency? Does the agency accept Medicare/Medicaid or reimbursement or only private pay? The answer to those questions reflects the philosophy of the agency and will influence pricing. Fees set by the agency must be compared with those of the competition to see if they are indeed competitive.

PROMOTION: The agency must first decide the objective it wants to achieve, such as to increase the public awareness or to increase clients usage of the services. Once you have determined the objectives, the agency needs to question how to design advertising material that supports the objectives.

PLACE: Most agencies do not have to worry about clients coming to them, but do need to think about employees coming into the agency. For a home care agency, just because the services are delivered exclusively in the client's home, does not mean that the physical office can be run down, neglected, or disorganized. It does mean that wherever the office is located it must be neat, well maintained, in order to provide quality service and avoid creating a negative image of the services offered.

PERSONNEL: Are the key to the creation of the services and its delivery to the clients in a consistency acceptable fashion. Clients associate traits of personnel with the traits of the agency with whom the service personnel are employed. This is particularly true for elderly home care agencies, where the services are provided in the home, away from the agencies physical place of business. It is possible that the client's only contact with the agency is the person rendering the aid. Therefore, for home care agencies not only is the selection of qualified personnel so important, the professional appearance demands of employees in contact with the clients are also critical to the image and marketing efforts of the agency.

The reality of today's home care world is that possessing the ability to provide home care services is not sufficient to guarantee an adequate livelihood for one's family or those of its employees. Today's world is one of limited resources. Marketing helps improve the odds that your agency will be able to earn its fair share of dollars.

MARKETING PLAN

A *marketing plan* is an unusual beast in the business world. There isn't a single accepted model that one can follow as there is with a business plan, nor has there been a lot written about marketing plans.

It is as much a process as a document that guides your agency in accomplishing their essential tasks. This is a combined research, analytical, and creative process, leading to development of strategy.

A marketing plan is a continuous process concerned with five phases:

- Obtaining commitment from management to carry out a market plan.
- Carrying out an audit of the internal and external environment.
- Formulating plans of identifying problems areas and develop strategies to achieve goals.

- Institute control to evaluate performance and modify plan.

MARKETING PLAN vs BUSINESS PLAN

Planning is essential if home care agencies are to meet the challenges of the rapidly changing home care market. The marketing plan provides you with these additional benefits.

- Stimulates thinking to use resources
- Assign responsibilities
- Sets schedule
- Coordinates efforts
- Facilitates control and evaluation
- Creates awareness of obstacles
- Identifies marketing opportunities
- Provides information sources
- Leads to achieving agency's goals.

DEVELOPING A MARKETING PLAN

A plan doesn't just happen. A system to create a market plan must be designed to meet the agency's requirement. A market plan is a continuous process that can be added to quarterly, yearly, or at whatever interval the agency sets up.

The marketing plan has seven components:
- Executive Summary
- Background Information
- Objectives & Goals
- Marketing Strategies
- The Scope of Work
- Budget
- Control

Each of the above components will now be discussed individually:

EXECUTIVE SUMMARY: The executive summary is a brief overview of the market plan. It explains why the marketing plan was prepared; list the major conclusions and recommendations. It is designed to give a quick overview of the marketing efforts and should be no more than one to two pages long.

BACKGROUND INFORMATION: This material should summarize prevailing conditions and other important observations. For example, data on the activity of the agency would be appropriate: a) income from Medicare/Medicaid b) number of visits c) major types of clients d) services rendered e) source of referrals.

Following those data's, strengths and weakness should then be listed. The list of strengths helps identify the base on which to build strategies. While the list on weakness allows the agency to recognize items that need correcting.

OBJECTIVES AND GOALS: Setting objectives and goals involves looking ahead and describing the desires of the future. Specific goals and objectives should be set that reflects the desired future in operational terms.

MARKETING STRATEGIES: The market plan describes the actual strategies that will be implemented. Information is needed about the rational for each strategy and the steps or procedures necessary to carry it out.

SCOPE OF WORK: A chart should detail the tasks that need to be undertaken, including the resources needed, sequences, and due dates of each task. Due dates can be specified by week, month, ore year, depending on the complexity of the model.

BUDGET: Based on the goals and objectives and strategies the agency has selected the budget is presented. The budget includes a detailed account of

direct cost, labor, overhead, administration expenses, profit or fees, and total project cost.

CONTROL: This is the last section of the plan and it describes the system of control that has been developed. A control system is established to maximize the probability that the short-term objectives of the agency will be met. The control phase concerns whether and how well the objectives and goals were achieved. After these questions are answered the agency will know that actions must be taken to improve the results.

CHAPTER 8

Staffing
The Agency

Once the functions and organizational structure are defined, competent personnel must be found. Recruiting and maintaining competent staff, individuals who are well trained for their respective positions and able to work as team members are factors in the successful operation of an elderly home care agency. The investment in time, money and energy placed in recruiting, hiring and training staff will reduce turnover and "pay off" over the years.

Staffing is a management functions that involves several aspects of administration: developing staff recruitment procedures, hiring, training, directing, evaluating, promoting and terminating.

RECRUITMENT

It is well to remember that recruitment is distinct from hiring in that it refers to the process and methods of appraising people of the employment opportunity and attracting them to the position. Developing effective recruiting techniques is especially important in the field of Elderly Home Care Services, because you will mainly be using C.N.A'S, Homemaker-Aide's, and Sitters, who often know little about the service and what they actually do. Another factor is that the potential population from which employees are recruited do not necessarily consider themselves to be in the labor market. Women for instance, who have been homemakers in their own home for many years may not see the opportunity for a second career until it is called to their attention. Creatively reaching out and educating the community will help attract competent, mature people who can be trained as good workers.

Several aspects of the work should be emphasized in developing recruiting materials. One for instance, is that employment as a homemaker or sitter offers men and women a career opportunity in which they can use their skills, talents, and life experiences. Another should be to depict the positive effects of the service, such as the fact that the sick or elderly are able to remain in their own homes as a result of their work.

The recruitment process and procedures of a home care agency may vary by the type of agency, size, organization structure and locale. Home care agency may encounter both *"feast and famines"* when attempting to attract new employees.

HOW TO FIND EMPLOYEES:

The search for new employees in a home care agency may include: advertising in newspaper, from school, and through the agency's own employees who attract qualified workers among their own families, friends and acquaintances.

SELECTION OF EMPLOYEES

The selection of qualified and competent personnel should be the results of a planned, formalized procedure, not arbitrary or casual decision. A formal selection process increases the likelihood that the requirement for knowledge, skills, and capabilities will be identified for each position. It also will mean that agencies having one or more staff persons interview, should check references and assure that health examination have been conducted recently.

Several steps maybe identified in a formalized selection process:

Completion of Application form: Each applicant should complete an application form and material recommended by the equal employment opportunity commission. The application educational and work history, skills and training, references, and other information must be obtained.

Initial Screening: The application form should be reviewed. If the applicant appears to be qualified and interested, a interview should be arranged.

Interview: One or more appropriate staff members jointly or independently can conduct the personnel interview. It should lead to an assessment of the applicant personal qualifications, as well as allow for a more thorough exploration of the applicant's experience and expertise. The interviewer should use a guide to be sure that all relevant points are covered.

Outlined below is the type of information to be sought in the interview. Throughout the interview, one should be sensitive to an applicant potential: personality and motivation are more important than formal education.

- The applicant's reason for wanting to work for you.
- The applicant's preferences for working with specific groups.
- The degree to which the applicant can accept working in some home conditions
- The ability to communicate
- The capacity for tolerance and understanding of different life styles and cultures.
- A sense of humor
- The readiness to acquire new relationship
- The readiness to learn new skills and to participate in training programs.
- Physical mental health and the sense of well-being.

Review of Reference: If after the interview, the applicant seems qualified and continues to be interested, the agency should request personal and employment references.

Health Examination: Local ordinances should be checked regarding specific requirement. Even if not required a health examination is recommended as a condition for employment. An up-to-date health examination record indicates that the agency's effort to do all that was possible to protect its staff and its clients.

Final Decision and Informing the applicant: The decision to hire an applicant may be solely by the person responsible for hiring or it can be made in consultation with the executive director.

Probationary period and evaluation: The selection process is never full-proof. An agency's staffing procedures should include a formal performance review which should be conducted at the end of the probationary period and result in regular employment, continued probation or dismissal. The term of the evaluation should be clear to the employee at the outset.

Performance review: Quite often especially in smaller agencies, evaluation, if they take place at all are informal.

Nevertheless, there are advantages to periodic performance reviews. An employee unaware of an inadequate performance which could lead to dismissal, should be alerted through performance review and given opportunity to improve her/his work and retain employment. Moreover, performance reviews can be used, in addition to agency and service assessments as a basis for formulating objectives for the ensuring year's work.

Personnel Policies and Procedures: A personnel manual should define clearly the rights and responsibilities of both the employer and employee regarding working conditions, hours, compensation, fringe benefits, and promotion polices. All personnel should be supplied with a copy of this manual.

Orientation: An orientation of all personnel should be provided at the outset of employment. The amount of time used and type of material presented may differ depending on the category of personnel.

Rate of Pay: Pay should be commensurate to the responsibilities. Appropriate pay scales can be determines by inquiring into pay scales of comparable agencies.

Scheduling Staff: The scheduling of home care service staff is one of the most complex areas. Even the best laid plans are subject to many and frequent changes due to rapidly changing needs of individuals being served and the availability of personnel. The scheduling functions must be carried out so that: personnel are efficiently deployed; those who need service receive them in a timely manner; records are maintained accurately with date, time and type of service provided.

Personnel Records: A record of employment should be maintained for every worker in the agency. The personnel records serve as a history of the workers background and experiences from the beginning of employment until termination.

{Records should be maintained for at least five years after termination of employment.}

PART III

Financial Management

CHAPTER 9

Financial Management

The **management** of a home care agency consists broadly of two functional areas: **operations** and **finance.** The ongoing operations of the agency consist of providing service and the financial functions consist of monitoring service cost and keeping adequate records. Clearly the financial functions are an integral part of the operations.

All operating policies and decisions have financial ramifications. The decision to hire additional staff will depend upon the availability of funds to absorb the increased costs. The expansion of a program will depend on the availability of new funds or the shifting of costs from some programs to new programs.

Financial management therefore is the recognition of the impact that finances has on the agency and the development of policies, procedures, and systems to monitor that impact.

BUDGET

As one would expect from looking at the objectives, the sources required to prepare the annual budget comes from all functional activities in the agency.

The starting point for determining the anticipated costs of services is to assess the demand for services. This demand should be expressed in hours of service or number of visits needed by the community. After the agency has been in operation for at least a year, the previous year experience plus any new services planned will be the starting point for the planning activity.

The next step is to prepare staffing and cost estimates, required to meet the level of services anticipated. Don't forget to include 20-25 percent or more of gross salaries for the cost of employee's benefits such as employer's share of Social Security Taxes (FICA) as part of staffing costs. After all the staffing costs and related costs are estimated, supporting services (administration) are allowed to the project to develop unit costs of services. Planned revenues are added to the budget to determine whether adjustments in expenditures are required.

Preparing the budget is a dynamic process. The first draft when reviewed will precipitate a series of initial decisions which will create the need to prepare a second and possibly a third draft. The final budget will be arrived at when the plan is acceptable to the agency.

Elderly home care services are complex to administer particularly in relation to financial management and accountability. For this reason I have written a manual " **Systematic Approach to Financial Management for Home Care Agencies.**"

DEVELOPING A BUDGET FOR A
BEGINNING AGENCY

Sound fiscal management which involves both budgeting and accounting is essential to the survival of a home care agency. Budgeting is the process of planning and projecting expenses and income; accounting is the process of maintaining and monitoring a current written record of expenditures and income.

PREPARING A BUDGET

Two basic steps are involved in developing a plan of expenditures. Key personnel should be involved throughout the process.

Specifying Goals and Objectives: A step often overlooked in developing a new budget, is the determination of realistic goals for the following year, which should be based on community need and agency capacity.

Developing a Written Plan of Action: The next step is to determine how the objectives are to be accomplished, what resources are available, the tasks to be performed and what materials and supplies will be needed. A most critical step in this process is to assess realistically the sources and amount of income that may become available to the agency within the year. The plan of action that emerges from this process is the basis on which following years' expenses and income can be estimated.

When reviewing the budget a number of questions should be answered: Do we have the right number of people? Is our level of service acceptable? Are our prices competitive?

ANNUAL BUDGET

REVENUE	AMOUNT
Client Fee's	$50,000.00
Grant's	10,000.00
Gifts	2,000.00
Other's	500.00
Total Revenue	**$62,500.00**

EXPENSES:	
Salaries	$45,000.00
Payroll Taxes:	
FICA	3,200.00
Medicaid	650.00
Supplies	1,000.00
Telephone	1,200.00
Postage	600.00
Rent	5,450.00
Equipment	2,000.00
Insurance	800.00
Utilities	1,200.00
Printing	900.00
Misc.	500.00
Total Expenses	**$62,500.00**

METHODS OF ACCOUNTING

Using functional budgeting as a foundation, expense and income can be recorded in one or two ways; According to a system of accrual basis accounting, or cash basis accounting.

Accrual means that revenues are entered into the books as soon as the agency has earned it, regardless of when it is collected. Similarly, expenditures are recorded when liabilities are incurred not when they are paid.

Cash basis accounting, revenues and expenditures are recorded when they are received or paid regardless of when they occurred. Cash reporting provides the potential for manipulation. The law requires accrual reporting in many areas.

AGENCY RECORD-KEEPING

There is a basic set of records, which all agencies should maintain though the scope and size of them will vary from agency to agency. They are a journal and a ledger. Records can take many forms. Today computer programs are economically feasible to assist in the record-keeping for small and large business. The level of details maintained can vary, but generally the data which should be recorded include: date of transaction; dollar amount, name and description of transaction.

FORMS AND SOURCE DOCUMENTS

The number of forms and source documents used by an agency is high. A representative list includes:

Vendor invoice	Purchase order
Billing invoices	Time report sheet

TAXES

For most small business, this subject is unpleasant to contemplate. Yet payment of these taxes is the lawful responsibility of every business owner. Failure to comply can lead to penalties, fines or worse.

Here are some common types of taxes your business maybe responsible for: federal withholding taxes, FICA, Medicare, FUTA, and State income tax.

CALCULATING COST FOR SERVICE

Once an agency has established a reliable accounting system, it then can determine the cost of service per hour or per visit, the amount of which becomes the basis for budgeting and developing a client fee schedule.

Services usually are reimbursed on the basis of an hour of direct service delivery time, that is, the time that the employee actually spends in delivering services. It is critical that these as well as all other operating costs are calculated in the cost per hour.

Before you can set your fees for the services, you first must calculate your total cost for operation expenses. The following items should be included: salaries, payroll taxes, rent, utilities, telephone, postage, office supplies, equipment, advertising, etc.

Taking the total costs of operating expenses and divide it by the number of anticipated chargeable hours of services. This is essentially a simple calculation. Total operating expenses.....$50,000.00 Divide by $10.00 per hour = 5,000 You will need to provide 5,000 hrs of service at $10 per hour to meet operating expenses.

CHAPTER 10

Protecting
Your Business

Being in business involves some degree of risk. Many common risks, such as: fire and accidents, can have serious financial effects on the day to day operations of a business. While it isn't possible to avoid risks completely, with the proper insurance coverage you can protect your business from the severe financial losses resulting from these risks.

Because insurance can shield your business from financial disaster, you should begin thinking about insurance coverage before starting your business. The purchase of coverage enables your business to transfer its risks. In exchange for a fee, the insurance company accepts the risk that the business wishes to be protected against.

TYPES OF COVERAGE

The first step in risk management is to identify the kinds of risks your business face. Next you have to analyze the potential losses and come up with a strategy for protecting your business losses and come up with a strategy for protecting your business against them. Here are some of the main risks you may want to consider insuring your business against:

Liability Insurance: As the owner of your business you are responsible for the safety of your employees and clients. If a client falls, you may be liable for damages. Most liability policies cover losses stemming from bodily injury or property damage claims. Expenses of medical services are required at the time of the accident.

The actual amount that your policy will pay depends on both the limit per person provided for in it. You should have general and professional liability insurance.

General Liability and Malpractice Insurance: Necessary to protect the staff, and the agency against legal suits which may arise, for instance from a worker's negligence or from accidents.

Professional Liability Insurance: Covers injuries resulting from the rendering or failure to render professional service.

General Liability and Professional Liability Insurance should be purchased from the same insurance company to obviate loopholes in settlements. For example, there maybe problems in determining whether a person's fall was due to negligence of staff person's incompetence in handling the patient.

PROPERTY INSURANCE: Covers the values of physical structure, contents and rent that have been damaged or lost specified circumstances.

AUTOMOBILE LIABILITY: Insurance protects the agency from claims arising from any accidents involving an employee's privately owned automobile while it is being operated on behalf of the agency.

UMBRELLA LIABILITY: Insurance indemnifies the agency against costs incurred from bodily injury or property damages that are not covered in or are in excess of the underlying limit of the policies mentioned above.

FIDELITY BONDS: New business owners are unaware that on the average, thefts by employees far surpass business losses from any other form. Unless you or a member of your immediate family, handle all phases of your business operation, you should obtain fidelity bond protection.

Before an employee is bonded, the insurance company issuing the bond conducts a character investigation to determine whether anything is knows of past acts of dishonesty. Then, if the employee is deemed bondable, coverage is provided. If a prospective employee refuses to be bonded, this could be a tip-off that the applicant has something to hide. A *fidelity bond* is available in three formats: individual, schedule and blanket bonds.

WORKERS' COMPENSATION INSURNACE: The Law requires an employer provide employees with a safe place to work, hire competent workers, provide safe tools, and warn employee of existing danger. An employer who fails to do so is liable for damages, including claims for on-the-job injury.

Under Worker's Compensation Insurance, it pays all sums you are legally required to pay a claimant. One way to save money on this insurance is to make sure your employees are properly classified.

HEALTH INSURANCE: A major employee benefits is increasingly being provided by service agencies. The agency may choose to contribute part or the entire policy premium.

Appendix I

Contract
For
Service

WALKER'S HOME CARE, INC.

Contract For Service

In consideration for the services provided by Walker's Home Care, Inc. for:_____, I (we) agree to pay Walker's Home Care, Inc. at the rate of $_____ per hour; if services are provided on Holidays, and Sundays the rate will be $_____ per hour. A deposit of $_____ is required prior to the start of service. The deposit will be refunded if services are canceled according to the provisions set forth below.

Days of Assignment (Circle one's that apply)

Mon Tues Wed Thurs Fri Sat Sun

Time of assignment: From_____ To_____

Hours per day_____ Total hours per week_____

Type of Service: CNA   HHA   Sitter   H-HHA

Client will only be billed for time used. If client elects to CANCEL a shift or all of the services, client agrees to notify the office 4-hours in advance of shifts and 48-hours in advance of cancellation of services.

Client understands he/she are not o HIRE any employee assigned or any office employee of Walker's Home Care. If the client hires any employee(s) within six (6) months from the date of cancellation of this contract, the client will pay Walker's Home Care $1,000.00 as liquidated damages for its costs in replacing such worker.

Client understands if they are not satisfied with the employee assigned, Walker's will provide a replacement up to (3) times. Client understands he/she are not to pay the employee directly, Walker's will bill for services.

The rates in this contract will remain the same for (9) months, if the duties remain the same. If bills are not paid in a timely manner services will be interrupted or canceled.

Date:_____   _____

                                               Signature of client or representative

_____

Walker's Home Care- Agent

80

Appendix II

CLIENT
INTAKE
SHEET

CLIENT INTAKE SHEET

DATE_____

NAME_____

PHONE_____

ADDRESS_____

_____

AGE_____

RELATIVE_____

GENERAL INFORMATION

_____

_____

_____

_____

_____

_____

_____

BILL TO:_____

REFERRAL SOURCE_____

START DATE_____

ASSESSMENT DATE_____

TYPE OF SERVICE_____

RATE QUOTE_____FOLLOW-UP_____

DIRECTION TO HOUSE:

_____

_____

_____

Appendix III

ASSESSMENT FORM

ASSESSMENT

Name_____

Address_____

Phone_____D.O.B_____Age_____

Emergency contact person_____

Referred by_____

Client Condition_____

_____

_____

Services Required:

Personal	Homemaking	Miscellaneous
Bath___	Wash dishes___	Exercise____
Shampoo___	Meals_____	Grocery____
Dressing____	Laundry_____	Ambulation___
Oral Care____	Bed_____	Transfer_____
Toileting_____	Garbage____	Medication____
Feeding_____	Mop/Vac____	Vital Signs_____

Other services not listed above:_____

_____

_____

Medication:_____

_____

_____

Direction to home:_____

Type of service_____ Days/Hours_____

Assessment Date_____ Start Date_____

Payment info: Rate_____ Bill to:_____

84

Appendix IV

Employment
Contract

Walker's Home Care, Inc.

EMPLOYMENT CONTRACT

Acknowledgement   by
_____ (employee)   I
understand I am being employed by Walker's Home Care
in a temporary or part-time position only, and for such time
as my services are required. I understand that this may be
temporary and remain part-time and said employment
does not entitle me to any special consideration for
permanent or full-time employment.

I further understand that my temporary employment maybe
terminated at anytime without cause or pursuant to
disciplinary procedures set forth for permanent or full-time
employees.

I also understand that I am not eligible to participate in any
fringe benefit programs or retirement programs or any
other program available to permanent or full-time
employees.

In addition, if I accept assignment I will remain on the
assignment until a relief is given. If I walk off the
assignment, I will be terminated and any monies owed will
be held until the next scheduled pay- day.

If (3) assignments are refused, I will be removed from
employees list. If client accuses me of theft, my wages will
be held until a full investigation is completed. And I agree
to cooperate fully with the investigation.

If I solicit a client of Walkers to hire me directly, I will be
terminated immediately. If client is not satisfied with my
work, I will be replaced.

Employee Signature_____
Walker's Rep._____
Date_____

Appendix (V)(VI) (VII)

Job
Descriptions

CERTIFIED NURSES AIDE (C N A)

JOB DESCRIPTION

CNA'S performs three general services on the job: 1) personal care 2) basic nursing 3) incidental homemaking.

BASIC NURSING DUTIES:

- Take and record temp, pulse, respiration, blood pressure
- Observe that patient follow medical orders
- Assist with self administered drugs
- Assist with prescribed exercise and mobility devices
- Perform simple urine test
- May restrain patient
- Give enema's
- Apply binders
- Treat decubiti
- Post mortem care
- Irrigate indwelling catheters
- Administer oxygen by cannula mask
- Intake and output

PERSONAL CARE:

- Bath
- Mouth care
- Feed patient

4) Shampoo
5) Shave
6) Turn patient

INCIDENTAL HOMEMAKING:

1) tidy bedroom
4) Wash dishes

2) Make bed
5) Meals

3) Dust/vac
6) Laundry

HOMEMAKER- HOME HEALTH AIDE
H-HHA

JOB DESCRIPTION

Perform duties such as: personal care, housekeeping, home management and emotional support.

- Making the home clean, safe and hazard free
- Shopping for food
- Planning and managing a household budget
- Light cleaning (dust, vacuum, wash dishes, etc.)
- Planning and cooking meals
- Do laundry
- Light help with personal care

- Assist with bath
- Take and record temp, pulse, resp.
- Back-rub
- Turn patient
- Assist patient to chair, bed, wheelchair

NOTE: SOME BASIC NURSING TASKS

SITTER OR COMPANION
JOB DESCRIPTION

SITTER/COMPANIONS MAIN JOB IS BEING A FRIEND

- Read, talk, listen and engage the patient in hobbies or stimulating activities, easing loneliness and isolation.

- Take patient shopping, handle errands

- Assist patient from bed to chair

- Assist patient with walking

- Prepare light meals

- Feed patient when needed

- Assist with bath, oral care

NOTE: Sitters/companion may not administer or perform any basic nursing skills.

CLEINT SHOULD BE ABLE TO ASSIST WITH THE CARE. SITTERS ARE NOT TRAINED TO CARE FOR SERIOUSLY ILL CLIENTS.

Appendix VIII

BALANCE SHEET

A BLANK BALANCE SHEET
(FOR YOU TO USE)

YOUR AGENCY'S NAME _____

DECEMBER 31, 19_____

ASSETS

CURRENT ASSETS:

Cash on hand $_____
Cash in bank   _____
Account Receivable   _____
Prepaid expenses   _____

Total... $_____

FIXED ASSETS

Fixtures & Equipment   _____

Minus depreciation   _____

Total... $ _____

TOTAL ASSETS............................. $ _____

LIABILITIES

CURRENT LIABILITIES

Account payable $_____

Taxes payable   _____

Loans   _____

TOTAL CURRENT LIABILITIES...... $_____

NET WORTH............................. $_____

Appendix IX

Income Statement or Profit & Loss Statement

INCOME STATEMENT
PROFIT AND LOSS STATEMENT

DATE_____

GROSS SALES_____

OPERATING EXPENSES:

    Salaries   _____
    Utilities   _____
    Rent   _____
    Printing   _____
    Insurance   _____
    Advertising   _____
    Bad Debts   _____
    Telephone   _____
    Tax's   _____

TOTAL OPERATING EXPENSES   _____

NET INCOME (OR LOSS)   _____

GLOSSARY OF TERMS

Accounting: The system for recording financial transactions in books and verifying, analyzing, summarizing and reporting the information for use in planning and decision-making.

Accrual Basis Accounting: An accounting system that recognizes expenses when they are incurred and revenue when they are earned, rather than when cash changes hands.

Advantages: A factor conductive to success. The benefit of doing something.

Asset: A resource of measurable financial value that the organization owns, such as cash, securities, accounts receivable, land, building and equipment.

Attitude: A state of feeling or mind of carrying out what you want to do.

Business Plan: A business plan is a written plan for what is going to be done and who will do it. It convey your vision to others.

Budget: The financial plan of an organization or agency for a specified future period of time, usually a year, based on planned expenditures during that period and expected income for funding the plan.

Budgeting: A systematic calculative process of planning expenditures to achieve objectives, given relative costs, within the limits of an anticipated line of income.

Cash Basis Accounting: An accounting system that records only those events that involves the exchange of cash. It ignores transactions that do not involve cash, such as monies owed to or by the organization.

Contract: An agreement, usually a written one, between two or more persons which is enforceable by law.

Corporation: A corporation is a body of persons granted a Charter that legally recognizes them as a separate entity with its owns rights, privileges and liabilities.

EIN (Employer Identification Number) ; Required by the Government for all new business to identify the business.

Fees: Monies billed to a recipient of service in full or partial compensation for services.

Fictitious Name: A name used for a business other than your own name.

FICA: Initials used for the term Social Security Taxes.

Financial Management: Is the recognition of the impact that finances having on the business and the development of policies, procedures and systems to monitor that impact.

Funds: A fund is a segregated portion of the organization's assets, liabilities, fund balances, revenue.

General Partner: A form of limited partnership that assume unlimited liability for the business.

Grants: An asset given to the agency by an individual or organization with legal restriction sometimes quite specifics imposed upon its use.

Goals: A statement of a desired result toward which an effort is directed.

Home Care: A blend of health and social services provided to individuals in their places of residence for the purpose of promoting, maintaining or restoring health or of minimizing the effects of illness and disability.

Liability: A claim on the assets of the agency by an outsider representing a financial obligation.

Limited Partnership: Is a form of partnership which the liability is confined to the amount of the investment and cannot take part in the management of the business.

Long-Term Goals: Are those things you want to accomplish three or more years into the future.

Marketing: If the process or mind set that focuses the business's efforts and actions on identifying and meeting the client's needs and wants.

Mission Statement: Is a long term vision of what the business is striving to become.

Partnership: Two or more people who have contracted to set-up a business.

Recruitment: Is the process and methods of appraising people of the employment opportunity and attracting them to the positions.

Referral: The process of bringing individual requiring services into contact with the appropriate agency.

Revenue: Assets obtained by the agency resulting in an increase in the appropriate fund balance.

Scheduling: The assignment of employees to cover the service required.

Short-Term Goals: Things you want to accomplish in less than a year.

Sole Proprietorship: A form of business in which one individual owns the business.

Working Capital: If the money you will need to tide you over until the business make enough money to cover its own expenses.

RESOURCES

Foundation Grants: Greater N.O.Foundation, 2515 Canal, St. New Orleans, La.

Personnel forms: James M. Jenks. Round Lake publisher Ridgefield Connecticut 1991

The Essential Book of Interviewing: By Arnold Kanter Times books New York 1995

Working from home: Paul and Sarah Edward, Jeremy P. Taracher, Inc. Los Angelas, Ca. 90069

Brickner P et.al The Homebound aged. A medically unreached group. Annals of Internal Medicine

Koester, Frances Planning and Setting objectives. New York, City, Public Relations Society of America.

Software:

Quick Books: Intuit , Inc. P.O. Box 34328 Seattle, Wa.

IRS PUBLICATIONS

Title	#
Employer's Tax Guide	15
Tax Guide for Small Business	334
Net Operating Loss	536
Accounting Periods and Methods	538
Tax Information on Partnership	541
Tax Information on Corporation	542
Taxpayers Starting a Business	583
Business Reporting	937
Basis of Assets	551
Tax information for S-Corporation	589
Guide for Free Tax Services	910

BO0K ORDER FORM

☐ How to Start an Elderly Home Care Business with the Change in your Pocket.................... $14.95

☐ Marketing Strategies for Home Care Agencies, Hospice Providers, Sitter & Elder Care Agencies......... $19.95

☐ Systematic Approach to Financial Management for Home Care Agencies................................$12.95

☐ Step-by-Step Guide for Starting & Running a Child Care Business.....................................$19.99

☐ Guide for Starting and Operating an Elderly Residential Care or Personal Care home.......................$19.99

☐ Policy & Procedure Manual for Adult Day Care $24.99

ADD $1.50 (Per Book) SHIPPING AND HANDLING to the above prices.

Mail check or money order to:

G. M. Walker
P.O. Box 16977
Jackson, Ms. 39236
Website:
www.booksbywalker.com

NOTES